This book belongs to ★

....

....

....

To Roderick,
Katrina and Andrew
from M.M.

Book design by Tracey Cunnell

Published in paperback in 1996
First published in Great Britain in 1994
by Orion Children's Books
a division of the Orion Publishing Group Ltd
Orion House
5 Upper St Martin's Lane
London WC2H 9EA

A catalogue record for this book
is available from the British Library
Printed in Italy
ISBN 1 85881 327 1

HOW TO COUNT
CROCODILES

Margaret Mayo
Pictures by Emily Bolam

CONTENTS

SOMETHING ABOUT THE STORIES

All the stories in this book have their roots in folk tale. Most of them have been freely adapted and retold from more than one source. 'How to Count Crocodiles' is from Indonesia and Japan. 'Father Bear and the Naughty Bear Cubs' is a Russian story found in *The Book of the Bear* by J. Harrison & H. Mirrlees (1926). 'Tortoise's Flying Lesson' is a fable from Aesop, but also comes from J.C. Harris *Daddy Jake and the Runaway* (1890). 'The Very Small Tabby Cat' is based on a Black American story in *Stars Fell on Alabama* by Carl Carmer (1934). 'Grandmother Rabbit and the Bossy Lion' is an Indian, African and Afro-American story. 'Why the Bluebird is Blue and the Coyote is Grey' is a North American Indian tale, from Frank Russell *The Pima Indians* (1908). 'The Friendly Lion' comes from India and England. 'The Little Hares Play Hop, Skip and Jump' is from Africa.

How to Count Crocodiles

Once there was a monkey who was always up to tricks and getting into mischief. There was no stopping her.

One morning she came dancing down to the river, and the first thing she saw, way over on the other side, was a mango tree laden with greeny-yellowy-orange mangoes. Just looking at those mangoes made her feel hungry.

"I must have some!" she said. "I must! But how can I cross to the other side?"

The monkey sat and she thought. And then...she saw a dark snout and two slit eyes, floating down the river.

"That's an old Snapper-jaws, if I'm not mistaken," she said. "He could be useful." She called out, "King Crocodile! GREAT King Crocodile!"

The crocodile lifted his head out of the water. "Are you talking to me?" he asked.

"I was, King Crocodile," she answered.

The crocodile grinned and showed every one of his white pointy teeth. He liked being called King Crocodile.

"I have been thinking," said the monkey. "There are lots of crocodiles living round here. But, even so, I bet there are more monkeys. Lots and lots more."

"Not so!" said the crocodile. "There are lots more crocodiles than monkeys!"

"We could do some counting," said the monkey, "and find out."

"And how could we do that?" asked the crocodile.

"Well," said the monkey, "you could go up and down the river and tell all the crocodiles to come here. Then I could do the counting."

"After that, you could get all the monkeys to come," said the crocodile, and he grinned again. "And we could ea... I mean...count them."

Then the crocodile swam up and down the river, telling his relations to come to a Big Crocodile Count.

"Because," he said, and he grinned yet again, "after that there is going to be a Big Monkey Count!"

The crocodiles didn't wait to be told twice, and it was not long before there was a great big tangle of crocodiles, twisting and turning, in the river near where the monkey sat.

At last the old crocodile himself arrived. "Everyone is here," he announced. "Let the counting begin!"

"ALL YOU CROCODILES!" shouted the monkey.

"GET IN A ROW! SIDE BY SIDE!"

And the crocodiles swam around until they had made a row that reached from one river bank right across to the other.

"ALL YOU CROCODILES! KEEP STILL!"

shouted the monkey, and she jumped on the back of the nearest crocodile and counted, "ONE!"

She jumped on the next crocodile. "TWO!" Then the next, and the next. "THREE! FOUR!" She kept on jumping and counting until she counted "TWENTY-NINE!" and with one last jump she was on the other side of the river.

She danced over to the mango tree. She climbed it, reached out, picked a greeny-yellowy-orange mango, and took a big bite.

"Ooooooh!" she said. "This mango is *sc-rum-ptious!*"

The old crocodile called out, "So there are twenty-nine crocodiles in this part of the river!"

"That's the number I counted," said the monkey.

"Now," said the crocodile, "go and fetch all the monkeys and line them up along the bank so I can count them."

"Go and fetch all the monkeys?" she said. "I wasn't planning to do that!"

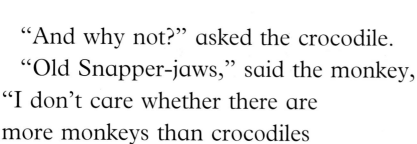

"And why not?" asked the crocodile.

"Old Snapper-jaws," said the monkey, "I don't care whether there are more monkeys than crocodiles or more crocodiles than monkeys. I only wanted to cross the river so I could eat some mangoes, and all you crocodiles make quite a good bridge when you get in a row, side by side!"

And she reached out and picked another greeny-yellowy-orange mango and bit into it.

Then twenty-nine angry crocodiles went swimming off to look for their dinner. And, to this day, what crocodiles like to eat most of all is... *monkey!* The trouble is monkeys are very, *very* hard to catch.

Father Bear
and the
Naughty
Bear Cubs

Once upon a time there was a Father Bear who lived in a cave with his two little bear cubs.

Every day Father Bear had to go into the forest to hunt for food, and every day, while he was away, the little bears were naughty. They splashed in puddles until they looked like wet washing. They wandered off and got lost. They growled and they quarrelled.

One day, when their father had gone hunting, the two little bears went for a walk in the forest. By and by, they came to a muddy patch, and—guess what they did. They jumped

SPLOSH! straight into the mud and stomped about

SQUISHY-SQUASHY!
SQUELCH! SQUELCH!

until they looked like two sticky mud cakes.

After a while, Grandmother Fox came trotting along. "You naughty bears!" she said. "What will your father say when he sees you?"

But the little bears laughed and sang out, "We don't care! Old Granny Bushy-tail, we don't care!"

Grandmother Fox was very cross. "I shall tell your father about you," she said. And she did just that.

"Oh dear! oh dear!" sighed Father Bear. "I must find someone to take care of my little bears while I am away. They are much too young and foolish to be left on their own."

So, next morning, Father Bear filled a sack with honey cakes, slung it over his shoulder, and walked off into the forest. He had not gone far when he met a black crow.

"Where are you going with a sack on your back?" said the black crow.

"I am looking for someone to take care of my little bears while I am away from home," said Father Bear.

"And what's in the sack?" asked the black crow.

"Honey cakes," said Father Bear. "Three honey cakes a day are the wages."

"For three honey cakes a day, I'd take care of them," said the black crow.

"Ah! but would you know how?" said Father Bear. "They can be very naughty."

"Of course I know how," said the black crow.

"I'd open my sharp beak and screech, CAW! CAW! CAW! That would soon make them behave."

"Black crow," said Father Bear, "you are not the sort of person I am looking for. You would frighten my little bears."

Father Bear walked on, and before long he met a grey wolf.

"Where are you going with a sack on your back?" said the grey wolf.

"I am looking for someone to take care of my little bears while I am away from home," said Father Bear.

"And what's in the sack?" asked the grey wolf.

"Honey cakes," said Father Bear. "Three honey cakes a day are the wages."

"For three honey cakes a day, I'd take care of them," said the grey wolf.

"Ah! but would you know how?" said Father Bear. "They can be very naughty."

"Of course I know how," said the grey wolf. "I'd show them my sharp teeth and howl *owww! owww! owww!* That would soon make them behave."

"Grey wolf," said Father Bear, "you are not the sort of person I am looking for. You would frighten my little bears."

Father Bear walked on, and before long he met a brown hare.

"Where are you going with a sack on your back?" said the brown hare.

"I am looking for someone to take care of my little bears while I am away from home," said Father Bear.

"And what's in the sack?" asked the brown hare.

"Honey cakes," said Father Bear. "Three honey cakes a day are the wages."

"For three honey cakes a day, I'd take care of them," said the brown hare.

"Ah! but would you know how?" said Father Bear. "They can be very naughty." "Of course I know how to take care of little bears," said the brown hare. "I would say

HUSH! HUSH! HUSH!

Then I would play with them and tell them stories. And if they were cross, I would tickle their tummies, and when they were tired, I would cuddle them close."

"Brown hare," said Father Bear, "you are just the sort of person I am looking for. You will love my little bears, and they will love you."

"But first I must look at those honey cakes!" said the brown hare.

Father Bear put the sack on the ground and opened it, and the brown hare poked in her head and she *sniff-sniff-sniffed!*

"Those are good honey cakes!" she said. "And three a day will suit me fine."

"Then that's agreed!" said Father Bear.

He slung the sack over his shoulder and made for home, and the brown hare leapt along beside him.

When they reached the cave, Father Bear said to his cubs, "Here is the brown hare. She will take care of you when I am away from home. So listen to her and try to be good."

"Oh! we will try!" said the little bears. "We will!"

After that, whenever Father Bear went off to hunt for food in the forest, the brown hare took care of the little bears. She played with them and told them stories. She tickled their tummies and cuddled them close. Every single day.

And the little bears listened to what she said, and they tried to be good. At least... most of the time, they did!

Tortoise's Flying Lesson

One hot, sunny day a tortoise was crawling along, slow and steady, when he saw an eagle up in the sky.

The eagle floated and flew, swooped and climbed, so light and easy that the tortoise thought, "I think I'll learn to fly! It looks like fun—especially when the sun is hot!"

Next morning the tortoise crawled up to the rocky place where the eagle had his home and said to him, "Eagle, please will you teach me to fly?"

"Fly? You think you can fly?" laughed the eagle. "You haven't any feathers. Besides—"

"Feathers! I forgot about feathers," said the tortoise. "I'll have to do something about that." And he went crawling off.

First he found some treacly gum, oozing out of a tree, and he smeared the gum over his shell.

Then he called on all his feathered friends—

the woodpecker,

kingfisher,

magpie

and dove,

the blackbird,

sparrow,

robin

and wren,

and lots more besides—

and he said to each of them,

"If you are my friend,

will you please give me a feather?"

And each bird gave the tortoise a feather—and he just stuck
those feathers on his shell, until he looked like a big feathery ball!

And *then* he crawled along, slow and steady, back to the eagle's rocky place.

"I've got the feathers," said the tortoise. "So now, will you please teach me to fly?"

"Tortoise!" said the eagle. "Feathers are not enough! You're just not the right shape for flying. There's too much of you in one place."

"Me? Not the right shape for flying? Nonsense!" The tortoise was cross. "If you are my friend, eagle, you will teach me to fly!"

31

The eagle shook his head. "I can't do that," he said. "But I can give you a ride." And he leant sideways so that the tortoise could climb up.

When the tortoise was settled and comfortable, he called out, "The flying lesson can begin!"

Then the eagle spread his wings and sailed up and up and up.

When he was almost as high as the clouds, he floated and flew, he swooped and climbed. Round and round, in circles.

"*Wow-eee!*" whooped the tortoise. "This is fun. I haven't had a ride like this before!"

Well, the eagle gave the tortoise a long ride before he sailed down and landed.

"Thank you," said the tortoise, as he slid off the eagle's back. "When can I have another lesson?"

"I'll give you a ride tomorrow," said the eagle. "Same time. Same place."

So next day the tortoise had another ride: and the tortoise kept on asking and the eagle kept on giving him a ride, day after day.

After a week, the tortoise said, "Eagle, I reckon I'm ready to do some flying on my own."

"And how are you going to take off?" asked the eagle.

"Taking off is hard," said the tortoise. "I think you'll have to give me some help with that."

Once again, the tortoise climbed on to the eagle's back, and they sailed up and up and up. When they were almost as high as the clouds, the eagle said, "Are you sure you want to fly?"

"Of course I'm sure!" said the tortoise. "I'm ready and eager!"

Then the eagle tipped sideways…and the tortoise slid off…

and began to fall...
down...
down...
down.

As he fell, his feathers blew off, this way and that. He flapped his feet, he waggled his head and he wiggled his tiny tail. But he went on falling. He flapped his feet, waggled his head and wiggled his tiny tail faster and faster, and with so much flapping, waggling and wiggling, he turned somersaults. So—when he reached the ground, he landed PLUNK! flat on his back.

His feathers were gone, and if he had not had such a tough shell, his body would have been all smashed to pieces. He was still lying where he landed, taking deep breaths, when the eagle flew down and flipped him right side up.

"How do you feel?" asked the eagle.

"I feel a bit of a wreck," said the tortoise.

"I warned you," said the eagle. "I knew you weren't the right shape for flying. I knew you couldn't do it!"

"What do you mean?" said the tortoise. "I flew! I flew a long way! Flying is as easy as falling! But landing...now, that *is* difficult. And the trouble was, my friend eagle, that you forgot to teach me how to land!"

The eagle laughed and laughed. He was so full of laughing he couldn't say a word.

But the tortoise took no notice. Holding his little head up as high as he could, he crawled off home, slow and steady.

And that was the very last time a tortoise tried to fly.

Grandmother Rabbit and the Bossy Lion

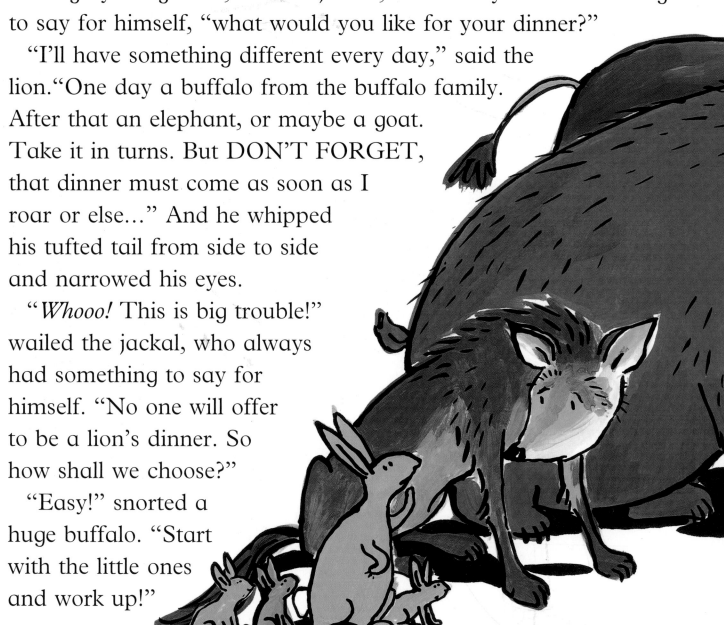

Long ago there lived a big, fierce lion who was very bossy and always had to have his own way about *everything*.

One day this bossy lion called a meeting of all the animals and told them that he had decided to be their king. "So, from now on," he said, "whenever I roar, you must bring me my dinner, or else…" And he whipped his tufted tail from side to side.

"Mighty King Lion," said a jackal, who always had something to say for himself, "what would you like for your dinner?"

"I'll have something different every day," said the lion. "One day a buffalo from the buffalo family. After that an elephant, or maybe a goat. Take it in turns. But DON'T FORGET, that dinner must come as soon as I roar or else…" And he whipped his tufted tail from side to side and narrowed his eyes.

"*Whooo!* This is big trouble!" wailed the jackal, who always had something to say for himself. "No one will offer to be a lion's dinner. So how shall we choose?"

"Easy!" snorted a huge buffalo. "Start with the little ones and work up!"

The big animals looked around, and their eyes rested on the rabbit family.

"All right," said Grandmother Rabbit, "if a rabbit has to go first, I will go. I won't send one of my children or my special little grandchildren!"

So it was decided that when the lion roared his hungry roar, Grandmother Rabbit would go and be his dinner.

The following morning, as soon as the sun was up, there was a loud lion's roar. *"HOOR-RR-RR!"*

Everyone in the rabbit family woke. But Grandmother Rabbit said, "It's too early to get up!" And they all closed their eyes and went to sleep again.

Time passed, and there was a louder, longer roar.

"HOOOOR-RR-RR!"

Everyone in the rabbit family woke. But Grandmother Rabbit said, "Breakfast time!" So they all hopped off and nibbled some juicy leaves.

Time passed, and then there were a whole lot of very loud, very long roars. *"HOOOOR-RR-RR!*

HOOOOR-RR-RR!

HOOOOR-RR-RR!"

But Grandmother Rabbit just wiggled her nose and nibbled some more juicy leaves.

Then from every direction animals came running—elephants, buffaloes, deer, sheep, goats, jackals. They were all shouting: "The lion is getting angry! Grandmother Rabbit—go! go! go!"

"All right," said Grandmother Rabbit. "I'm off. See you soon."

The jackal, who always had something to say for himself, shook his head. "That is one very foolish rabbit," he said. "She is going to be a lion's dinner. And what does she say? *See you soon!*"

Grandmother Rabbit hopped along until she came to a well that had steep sides. She stopped and looked down. And when she saw her reflection in the water, she pricked up her ears, wiggled her nose, lifted her paw and gave herself a friendly wave. Then off she hopped.

The moment the bossy lion saw her, he roared, "You're late!"
He narrowed his eyes and looked more closely. "And you're too
small! You won't make more than a mouthful."

"King Lion, I know I'm small," said Grandmother Rabbit.
"But I was chosen, so I came. I would have been here earlier,
but another lion grabbed me on the way. He was going to eat
me, but I managed to run away."

"Who was he?" asked the lion.

"I've never seen him before," said Grandmother Rabbit.
"He was awfully big. Much bigger than you!"

"Bigger than WHO?" roared the lion.

"Maybe he was the same size," said Grandmother Rabbit. "But he was mighty fierce."

The lion whipped his tufted tail from side to side. "Take me to him!" he said.

"That other lion is so big and ferocious," said Grandmother Rabbit, "I'm afraid he might hurt you."

"Hurt WHO?" roared the lion. "Take me to him! Now!"

So off hopped Grandmother Rabbit, and the lion padded along behind. And where did she take the bossy lion?

She took him to the well.

When they got there, she whispered, "That-other-lion-is-in-there."

The bossy lion padded over to the well and looked down into the water—and there was a lion's face looking back at him! The bossy lion shook his mane and showed his teeth—and the other lion shook his mane and showed *his* teeth! The bossy lion roared, "Hoor-rr-rr!"—and the other lion echoed, "Hoor-rr-rr!" right back at him!

This made the bossy lion so angry that he jumped straight at the other lion and landed in the well!

Once he was in, he could see there was no other lion. There was only himself. But once in, he couldn't get out, because the sides of the well were steep and slippery. So he floundered about and swallowed water. And that was the end of him.

Then Grandmother Rabbit hopped off as fast as her legs could go.

When she reached home, her children and her special little grandchildren were so happy to see her again. And when she told them how she had tricked the bossy lion, they were very proud of their brave Grandmother Rabbit and made a big fuss of her.

As soon as the other animals heard the story, the jackal, who always had something to say for himself, shook his head and said, "Well, well, well, that is one very clever rabbit!"

And he was right.

The
Very Small
Tabby Cat

Once there was a very small tabby cat and she did not like being small. She wanted to be big.

She ate and she ate. But it made no difference. She didn't grow any bigger.

She humped her back. She stretched and she jumped. But it made no difference. She didn't grow any bigger.

So—she sat and she thought, and at last she said, "I know what I'll do! I'll ask some of the big animals what they did to make themselves big!"

Off she ran...and she met a horse.

"Friend horse," said the tabby cat, "tell me, please, what did you do to grow big?"

"Nothing much," he answered. "I ate lots of oats. I ran round a field about twenty times a day. And I just grew."

"I think I'll try that," said the tabby cat.

And she ran round a field twenty times and she ate lots of oats. But all the running made her little legs ache, and the oats made her stomach ache...and she didn't grow any bigger.

So—she sat and she thought, and at last she said, "Now I must ask some other big animals what they did to make themselves big!"

Off she ran...and she met a bull.

"Friend bull," said the tabby cat, "tell me, please, what did you do to grow big?"

"Nothing much," he answered. "I ate lots of grass. I bellowed *mooo-oooh!* about twenty times a day. And I just grew."

"I think I'll try that," said the tabby cat.

And she bellowed *"Mooo-oooh!"* twenty times, and ate lots of grass. But all the bellowing made her little throat sore, and the grass made her sick…and she didn't grow any bigger.

So—she sat and she thought, and at last she said, "Friend horse didn't help. And friend bull didn't help. Now what shall I do?"

Then she heard an owl hooting *"Hoo! hoo! hoo!"* way off in the woods.

"I know what I'll do," she said. "I shall go and see the wise owl."

Off she ran…and she found the owl, high up in a tree, blinking his big round eyes, open and shut, open and shut.

"Friend owl," said the tabby cat, "tell me, please, what must I do to grow big?"

The owl closed his eyes and opened them again. "Why do you want to be big?" he asked.

"I want to be big," said the tabby cat, "so that…well…if I get in a fight I can win."

The owl closed his eyes and opened them again. "Has anybody ever picked a fight with you?" he asked.

"No-o," she said. "I am friends with everyone."

"Then you don't need to be any bigger," said the owl.

"But I'm so small," said the tabby cat, "that I always, always, *always* have to look up at the other animals. And I'm tired of that. I'd like them to look up at me sometimes!"

The owl closed his eyes and opened them again. "Can you climb a tree?" he asked.

"Yes," she said. "I can."

"Then you don't need to be any bigger," said the owl. "When you want a big animal to look up at you—*climb a tree!*"

"I hadn't thought of that," said the tabby cat.

"It doesn't matter what size you are," said the owl. "Just use your brains, and you'll find you are big enough to do anything."

"Thank you, friend owl," said the tabby cat. "I think I'll try that."

So then—every day the very small tabby cat used her brains and she found that she was really, truly big enough to do anything she wanted.

Why the Bluebird is Blue and the Coyote is Grey

When the world was new and there was magic everywhere—in lakes and mountains, in rivers and rocks—in those times, the little bluebird wasn't blue. He was grey. And the coyote wasn't grey. He was green.

The little grey bird lived beside a lake, up in the mountains. It was a beautiful lake, always the same. Sunshine or rain, its water shone the bluest blue.

Every day the little grey bird flew round the lake, and he wished he was not such a dull grey colour, and he sang, over and over, "Blue, blue, I wish I was blue!"

The Spirit of the Lake heard his song, and one night when the bird was asleep, the Spirit of the Lake came and whispered in his ear: "If you want to be blue, jump in the lake, dip your head in the water and sing, *'Make me blue! Bluest blue water, make me blue!'* Every morning for four mornings you must do this, and then, little grey bird, you will see…"

When the little grey bird woke, he thought, "What a lovely dream!" And he flew down to the lake, jumped in the water, dipped his head and sang, *"Make me blue! Bluest blue water, make me blue!"*

Then he flew up. But he was still grey. The next morning and the next, he did the same thing. But he was still grey.

On the fourth morning, just as he jumped in the water, the coyote strolled by, hungry as usual and looking for something to eat. The coyote watched the little grey bird jump in the water and dip his head. The coyote watched him fly up...*and what was this?*...suddenly the bird was BLUE!

The coyote called out, "Hey! Bluebird! That was some magic! Tell me— how did you get to be blue?"

"Every morning for four days," said the first bluebird that ever was, "I jumped in the water, dipped my head and sang, *'Make me blue! Bluest blue water, make me blue!'* Then I flew up. And here I am, every feather the bluest blue!"

Then the bluebird flew off singing a happy song.

"That blue is the best colour ever," said the coyote. "I think I'll change from green to blue."

So he jumped in the lake, dipped his head and sang the song. He climbed up the bank, had a good shake and lay in the sun to dry. The next morning and the next, he did the same thing.

On the fourth morning the coyote jumped in the lake again, dipped his head and sang the song. He climbed up the bank...and he was BLUE! Every single hair was BLUE!

"What a colour!" he gasped. "I must go and show everyone. The wolf and the dog...they will be so jealous. The raccoon...

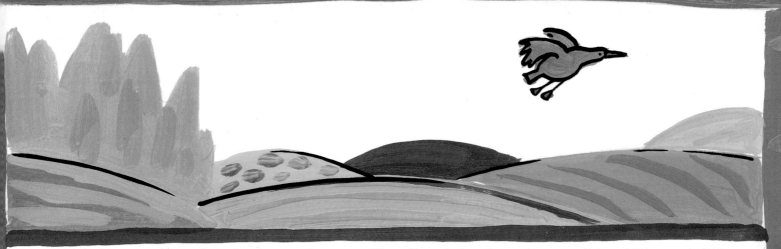

the possum…the bear…they will all wish they were blue like me!"

The coyote was in such a hurry to show everyone his new colour that he didn't wait to shake his coat dry. He just scooted off down the mountainside.

As he ran, he looked back at his blue tail and admired it. So he didn't notice the old tree stump, straight ahead, and he whammed into it, rolled over, and kept on rolling.

When he reached the bottom of the mountain, he was covered in dust. He scrambled to his feet and shook himself. He was still dusty. He shook himself some more. But the dust stayed.

After that, the coyote did a lot more shaking. But, no matter how many times he shook himself, or how many times he jumped in the lake, dipped his head and sang, *the dust stayed*.

Even today, the coyote has a scruffy coat. It is dusty grey all over. But the bluebird is still the bluest blue. He kept his magic colour.

The Friendly Lion

A timid mouse was lying fast asleep near a coconut tree when, all of a sudden, a coconut fell

PLOO-OOMP!

The timid mouse jumped up. "Oh! oh! The sky is falling!" he said. "I must go and tell the King!"

So he ran and he ran... and he met a shaggy dog.

"Where are you going?" asked the shaggy dog.

"Can't stop," said the timid mouse. "The sky is falling and I am going to tell the King."

"The sky is falling? Then I shall come too!" said the shaggy dog.

They ran and they ran…and they met a chattering monkey.

"Where are you going?" asked the chattering monkey.

"Can't stop," said the timid mouse. "The sky is falling and I am going to tell the King."

"The sky is falling? Then I shall come too!" said the chattering monkey.

They ran and they ran…and they met a dancing tiger.

"Where are you going?" asked the dancing tiger.

"Can't stop," said the timid mouse. "The sky is falling and I am going to tell the King."

"The sky is falling? Then I shall come too!" said the dancing tiger.

They ran and they ran…and they met a grumpy camel.
"Where are you going?" asked the grumpy camel.
"Can't stop," said the timid mouse. "The sky is falling and I am going to tell the King."
"The sky is falling? Then I shall come too!" said the grumpy camel.
Then ran and they ran…and they met a stupendously large elephant.
"Where are you going?" asked the stupendously large elephant.
"Can't stop," said the timid mouse. "The sky is falling and I am going to tell the King."
"The sky is falling? Then I shall come too!" said the stupendously large elephant.

They ran and they ran...and they came to a big cave.
The stupendously large elephant trumpeted, *"Aoo! Aoo!"*
The grumpy camel grumped, *"Hrumph! hrumph!"*
The dancing tiger growled, *"Grrrr! Grrrr!"*
The chattering monkey chattered,
"Jibba-jibba-jibba!" The shaggy
dog barked, *"Whoof! whoof!"*
And the timid mouse whispered,
"Snoofle-snoofle-snoofle!"
The King, who was asleep in
the cave, woke and he yawned.
Then he strolled outside.
He said, "WHAT IS ALL
THIS NOISE ABOUT?"

"King Lion," whispered the timid mouse, "I have come to tell you that the sky is falling!"

"The sky is falling? Surely not!" said King Lion, and he spoke softly and gently. "Look, there it is—up above!"

"But I heard it falling," whispered the timid mouse. "It went *PLOO-OOMP!*"

"Take me to the place where you heard the *PLOO-OOMP,*" said King Lion.

"But I am afraid to go back," said the timid mouse.

"No need to be afraid," said King Lion. "I shall look after you."

"But I am too tired to go back," said the timid mouse. "I have run such a long way."

"Climb on my back," said King Lion. "And I shall carry you there."

So the timid mouse climbed on to King Lion's back and told him the way to go.

And the lion bounded away...

and behind him ran the shaggy dog, the chattering monkey, the dancing tiger, the grumpy camel and the stupendously large elephant.

They ran and they ran… and they came to the coconut tree. Then the timid mouse jumped off King Lion's back, while all the other animals stood and stared.

"Timid mouse," said King Lion, "tell me again, what sort of noise did you hear?"

"It was a *PLOO-OOMP!* sort of noise," he whispered.

King Lion looked around, and he saw a coconut lying in the grass…and then he laughed a big lion laugh.

"No need to be afraid," he said. "It was a coconut you heard. Only a coconut falling from the tree and landing on the ground. There it is, lying in the grass."

"No need to be afraid," the other animals told each other. "It was only a coconut...only a coconut..." And they turned about and hurried off home.

"Now," said King Lion. "Time for a sleep. I am tired after all that running."

"Me too!" said the timid mouse.

The kind and gentle King Lion stretched out on the grass and closed his eyes, and the timid mouse curled up beside him. And very soon they were both fast asleep.

The Little Hares Play Hop, Skip and Jump

One day Mother Hare's little children were playing hop, skip and jump on a path through the jungly forest, when an elephant came trampling along.

As soon as he saw the little hares, he trumpeted:

"Out of my way! out of my way!
Or I'll trample you flat today, today!"

The little hares were so scared their hearts went *pit-a-pat! pit-a-pat!* and off they ran, until they came to a path by the river.

Then they huddled together, and when they had got their breath back, they began to play hop, skip and jump again. And then a hippo came trampling along.

As soon as he saw the little hares, he bellowed:

"Out of my way! out of my way!
Or I'll trample you flat today, today!"

The little hares were so scared their hearts went *pit-a-pat! pit-a-pat!* and off they ran, until they were safely home.

Then they told their mother how the elephant and the hippo had scared them.

Mother Hare was angry. "Those big animals should not scare my little ones," she said. "They must be stopped!"

Straightaway she hurried off, *jumpity-jump!* First she found some tough creeping vines and twisted them together to make a long rope. Then she went to see the elephant.

She said, "Big elephant, you scared my children today. And now I want you to promise *never, ever* to do that again!"

The elephant waved his stretchy trunk and trumpeted:

"I am big and I am strong,
So I'll do what I like, all day long!"

"You may think you are strong, big elephant," said Mother Hare. "BUT…if I tried, I could pull you out of this forest and down to the river!"

"Huh! I'd like to see you try!" said the elephant.

"Then let me tie this rope round your neck, and I'll show you who is the stronger," said Mother Hare.

So the elephant knelt down, and Mother Hare tied one end of the long rope round his neck.

"Now wait here until I shout PULL!" she said. "And then pull and pull, with all your strength."

With that, she hurried off, *jumpity-jump!* She came to the river, and there she found the hippo, wallowing in some shallow water.

She said, "Big hippo, you scared my children today. And now I want you to promise *never, ever* to do that again!"

The hippo opened his enormous mouth and bellowed:

"I am big and I am strong,

So I'll do what I like, all day long!"

"You may think you are strong, big hippo," said Mother Hare. "BUT...if I tried, I could pull you out of this river and into the forest!"

"Huh! I'd like to see you try!" said the hippo.

"Then let me tie this rope round your neck, and I'll show you who is the stronger," said Mother Hare.

So the hippo waded across to the river bank, and Mother Hare leant over and tied the other end of the long rope round his neck.

"Now wait here until I shout PULL!" she said. "And then pull and pull, with all your strength."

With that, she hurried off, *jumpity-jump!* into the forest. When she came to a place where the hippo and the elephant couldn't see her, she shouted, "PULL!"

The rope stretched until it was tight...and then a great pulling began. The elephant at one end pulled and he pulled. The hippo at the other end pulled and he pulled. The elephant gave a huge tug and jerked the hippo forward. The hippo planted his feet firmly in the muddy river, gave a huge heave and dragged the elephant forward. They moved forward and backward, forward

and backward…and they both grew more and more tired and weaker and weaker…until their strength was gone.

When it was almost evening, Mother Hare said, "The time has come to end this pulling game!" She picked up a sharp stone, rubbed it across the rope, and *twang!* it broke.

The elephant fell *plonk!* on his little tail, with his four feet in the air.

The hippo fell *splash!* into the muddy water.

And what did Mother Hare do? She hurried off, *jumpity-jump!* through the forest.

When she saw the elephant, she said, "It seems to me we are about equal when it comes to strength. So, big elephant, I want you to promise *never, ever* again to scare my children!"

"I promise," whispered the elephant. He was so tired he could scarcely speak.

Then Mother Hare untied the rope round his neck, and hurried off, *jumpity-jump!* through the forest, down to the river.

When she saw the hippo, she said, "It seems to me we are about equal when it comes to strength. So, big hippo, I want you to promise *never, ever* again to scare my children!"

"I promise," whispered the hippo. He, too, was so tired he could scarcely speak.

Then Mother Hare untied the rope round his neck, and hurried off, *jumpity-jump!* home to her little children.

From that time on, whenever the elephant and the hippo saw Mother Hare's little children, they walked softly along the path, and they spoke quietly, and they were always very polite.